HEAT

ANDREW DUNN

Illustrated by
ED CARR

Thomson Learning

New York

Titles in this series
Heat
It's Electric
Lifting by Levers
The Power of Pressure
Simple Slopes
Wheels at Work

Words in *italic* in the text are explained in the glossary on page 30.

First published in the
United States in 1993 by
Thomson Learning
115 Fifth Avenue
New York, NY 10003

First published in 1992 by
Wayland Publishers Ltd.

Copyright © 1992 Wayland Publishers Ltd.

U.S. version copyright © 1993 Thomson Learning

Cataloging-in-Publication Data applied for

ISBN 1-56847-018-5

Printed in Italy

Contents

What is heat?

How is the temperature where you are sitting? When you were outside, was it warmer or cooler? You know without thinking whether you are hot or cold. But what is heat?

Heat is a kind of *energy*. Everything in the world is made up of *atoms*, which cluster into *molecules*.

Heat energy makes molecules move and *vibrate*.

Inside everything, molecules are always moving slightly, even in the most solid rock. As an object gets hotter, its molecules vibrate faster. Cooling an object slows the molecules down.

The huge sun, 93 million miles away, provides most of the energy we have. Heat and light from the sun take eight minutes to get to Earth.

Most of the heat on Earth
comes first from the sun.
Waves of heat energy travel to
Earth in invisible *rays*.

H
E
A
T

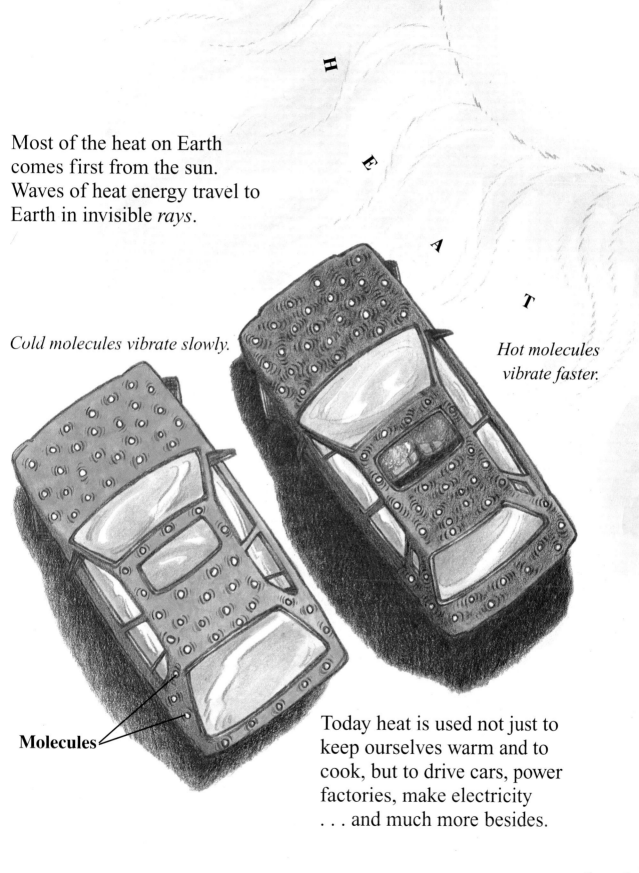

Cold molecules vibrate slowly.

*Hot molecules
vibrate faster.*

Molecules

Today heat is used not just to
keep ourselves warm and to
cook, but to drive cars, power
factories, make electricity
. . . and much more besides.

5

Heat on the move

Heat moves from one place to another, and always from a hotter place to a cooler one. It travels in three different ways.

Radiation

All hot objects radiate heat just like the sun. This means they give out heat in the form of rays. The rays are waves of energy, like light rays. The difference is that human eyes can see light rays, but not heat rays.

The rays themselves are not hot, but things become hot as the rays reach them.

Heat rays

Conduction

Heat spreads through liquids, gases, and some solids. The quickly vibrating, hot molecules bump into colder, slower molecules, making them vibrate faster and so heating them up.

Heat spreads

Convection

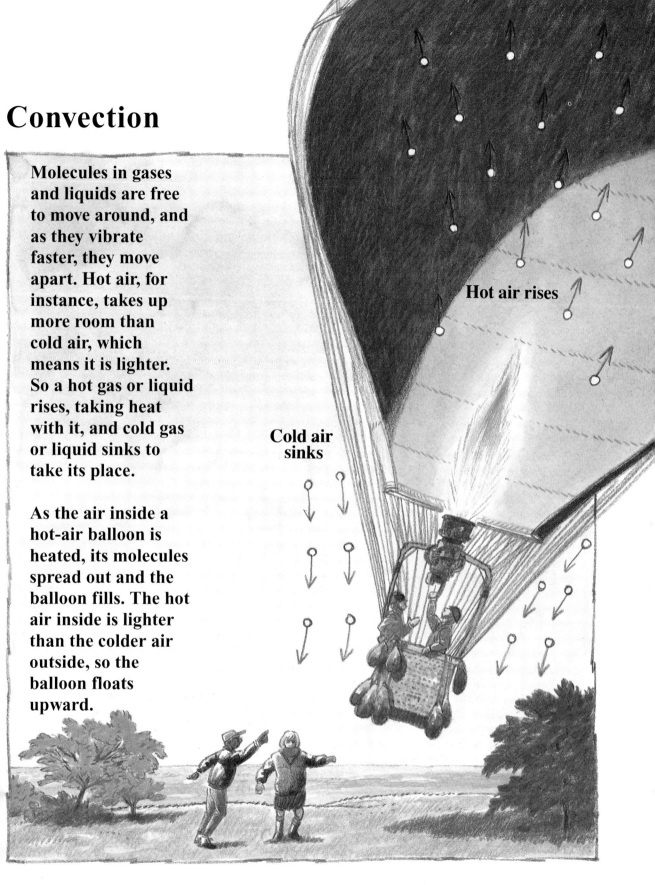

Molecules in gases and liquids are free to move around, and as they vibrate faster, they move apart. Hot air, for instance, takes up more room than cold air, which means it is lighter. So a hot gas or liquid rises, taking heat with it, and cold gas or liquid sinks to take its place.

As the air inside a hot-air balloon is heated, its molecules spread out and the balloon fills. The hot air inside is lighter than the colder air outside, so the balloon floats upward.

Hot air rises

Cold air sinks

Heat and temperature

Many people think "temperature" means "heat," but the two things are not the same. Two pints of water boiling in a pan has the same temperature as one pint, but twice as much heat. Heat is the total amount of energy in the pan. Temperature is how intense the heat energy is— how fast each single water molecule is vibrating.

Expansion and contraction

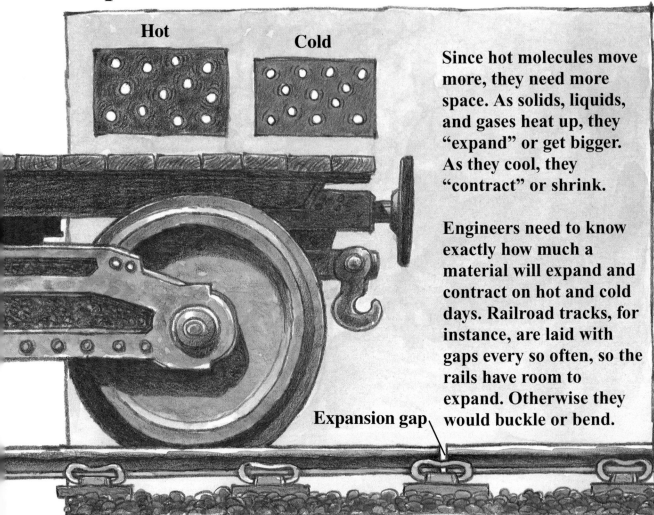

Hot

Cold

Since hot molecules move more, they need more space. As solids, liquids, and gases heat up, they "expand" or get bigger. As they cool, they "contract" or shrink.

Engineers need to know exactly how much a material will expand and contract on hot and cold days. Railroad tracks, for instance, are laid with gaps every so often, so the rails have room to expand. Otherwise they would buckle or bend.

Expansion gap

The thermometer

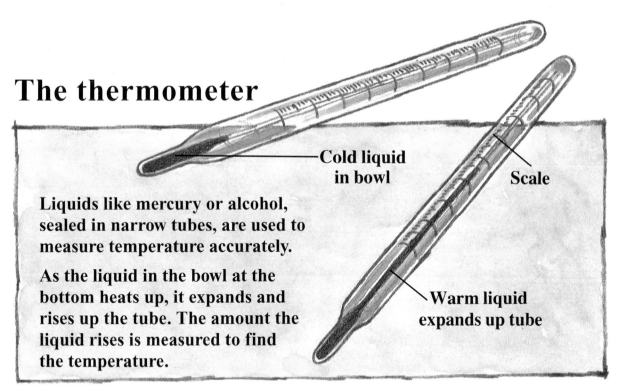

Cold liquid in bowl

Scale

Warm liquid expands up tube

Liquids like mercury or alcohol, sealed in narrow tubes, are used to measure temperature accurately.

As the liquid in the bowl at the bottom heats up, it expands and rises up the tube. The amount the liquid rises is measured to find the temperature.

Water is very unusual. Like other substances, it shrinks as it cools. However, unlike other substances, it expands when it freezes to form ice.

Heating for warmth

Ever since people first learned to control fire, they have used it to keep warm, to cook, and to provide light.

Fire results from the *combustion* of *fuel* (such as wood, coal, or gas) with air. This is a chemical process; in other words, it involves atoms.

Coal is made mainly of carbon. When coal burns, the molecules in it break up, and the carbon atoms combine with oxygen atoms from the air to make carbon dioxide. This process releases energy in the form of light and heat.

The combustion process

Oxygen + Carbon = Light Heat + Carbon dioxide

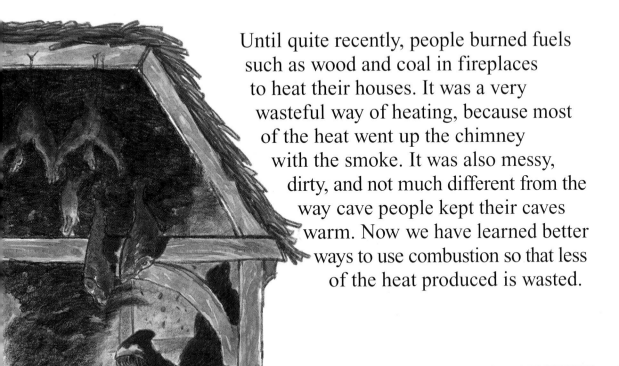

Until quite recently, people burned fuels such as wood and coal in fireplaces to heat their houses. It was a very wasteful way of heating, because most of the heat went up the chimney with the smoke. It was also messy, dirty, and not much different from the way cave people kept their caves warm. Now we have learned better ways to use combustion so that less of the heat produced is wasted.

Left *During combustion, carbon from fuel combines with oxygen from air to make carbon dioxide. During this process light and heat energy are released.*

Coals in an open fireplace burn red-hot, but the heat cannot be controlled. Coal also produces a lot of smoke.

Combustion and energy

Combustion can be used simply to produce heat. However, the energy combustion releases has a wide range of other uses, such as driving engines, making electricity, or joining metals together.

Welding

Pieces of metal can be joined together by *welding*. A very hot flame melts the metal. The liquid metal from each piece mixes, forming a strong bond as it cools.

The hot flame is made by burning a gas fuel (usually *acetylene*) with pure oxygen from pressurized cylinders.

Welding equipment can be used to bond metal.

The gas heater

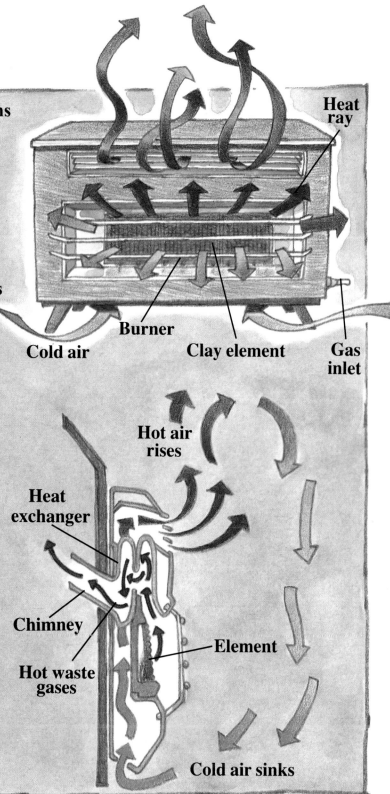

The way a gas heater burns gas means that most of the energy produced is used to warm the room. The heat travels all three ways—radiation, conduction, and convection.

Radiation: Cool air enters at the bottom, below the gas burners. The flames and the red-hot *elements*, made of a special clay, radiate heat into the room.

Conduction: The hot waste gases produced go up the chimney. Before they do, their heat is removed by conduction through metal panels in a "heat exchanger."

Convection: Heat from the heat exchanger warms air, which flows out and upward into the room by convection. As it does so, more cool air enters at the base.

Heat ray

Cold air

Burner

Clay element

Gas inlet

Hot air rises

Heat exchanger

Chimney

Hot waste gases

Element

Cold air sinks

13

Central heating

Not so long ago, the living room was the only warm room in many homes during winter. It was warmed by a stove, which was also used for cooking and heating water. People would take baths in tubs next to the stove. Today, central heating means that all the rooms in a house can be warm.

A boiler—burning gas, oil, or coal—is at the heart of a central heating system. Some systems blow hot air into rooms, while others heat water in small pipes. The hot water travels along the pipes to a hot-water tank.

The water is also piped to radiators around the house. "Radiator" is really the wrong word. A radiator heats a room by conduction and convection, not radiation.

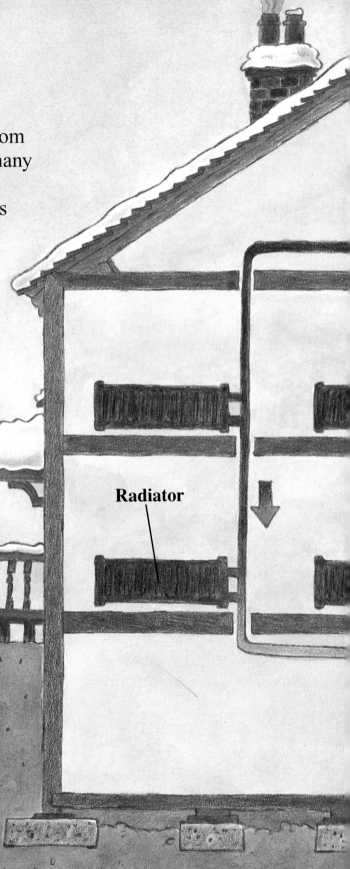

Radiator

Tank

Boiler

First the radiator warms the cold air next to it by conduction. As air warms, it becomes lighter and rises, drawing up more cold air from below and making a "convection current."

Hot water rises like hot air. This is one reason why the hot-water tank is usually upstairs and the boiler downstairs.

Water heated by the boiler rises and flows through the radiators. The radiators give off heat and the water cools.

The cool water sinks toward the boiler, ready to be heated again. In this way, hot water is constantly flowing through the pipes and radiators.

Electric heating

Electricity is a very useful form of energy. It is easy, instant, and clean to use (although the power plants that make it can produce a lot of *pollution*).

Electricity is a flow of particles, called *electrons*, which are even smaller than atoms. As they flow along a wire, they bounce against the atoms in the metal, which then vibrate more. The vibrations in the wire give off heat.

Heating elements are made of a special wire that makes the electrons work harder, which produces more heat.

Electricity flowing through the wires makes them red-hot. A shiny metal plate reflects heat rays outward.

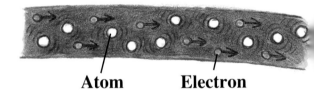

Atom   **Electron**

The electric heater

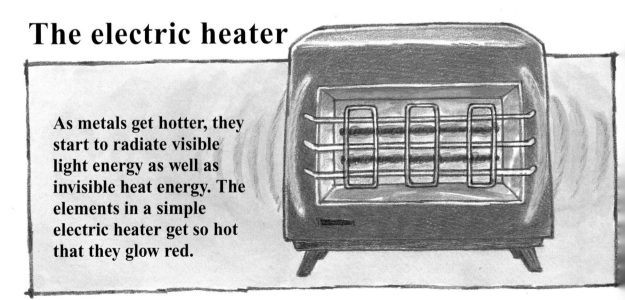

As metals get hotter, they start to radiate visible light energy as well as invisible heat energy. The elements in a simple electric heater get so hot that they glow red.

The storage heater

In some places, there are houses heated by storage heaters. These use electricity to heat up a material that holds on to heat, such as concrete or brick.

Once the bricks are hot, they release heat very slowly, keeping a room warm for hours.

Stoves, ovens, and thermostats

Electric stoves and ovens

Electric elements are used in stoves and ovens in different ways. The circular element of a stove heats a pot placed directly on it through conduction. Metal conducts heat very well.

The elements in an oven heat the air by radiation and convection. Since hot air rises, the hottest part of the oven is the top. Some ovens use fans to keep air moving and the temperature even at the top and bottom.

A stove heats a pan by conduction.

The thermostat

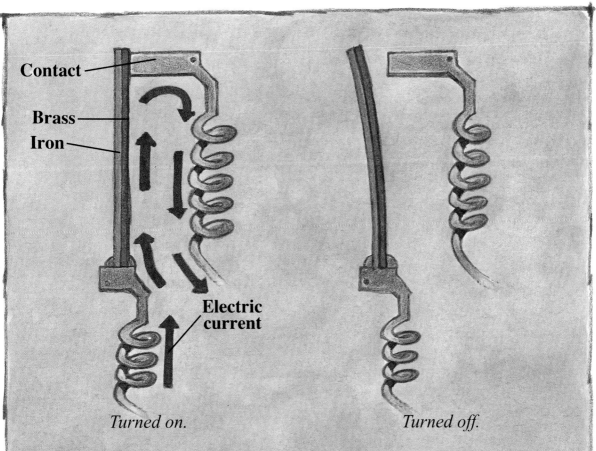

Contact

Brass

Iron

Electric current

Turned on.

Turned off.

A thermostat controls heat by turning electricity on and off. In an oven it turns the electricity off if the oven is too hot, and turns it on again when the oven cools. In a refrigerator, it works in the opposite way.

Everything expands as it gets hotter, but some materials expand faster than others.

One common type of thermostat is a strip made of different metals, such as brass and iron.

As it heats up, the brass expands more than the iron. So the strip bends, opening the switch and turning off the electricity.

As it cools, the strip bends back and turns the electricity on again.

The electric pot and the toaster

The electric pot

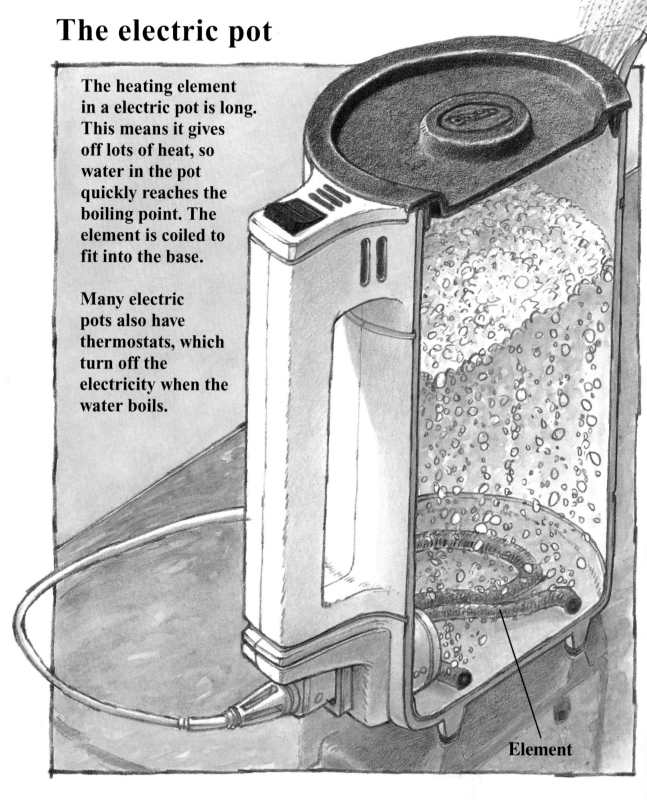

The heating element in a electric pot is long. This means it gives off lots of heat, so water in the pot quickly reaches the boiling point. The element is coiled to fit into the base.

Many electric pots also have thermostats, which turn off the electricity when the water boils.

Element

The toaster

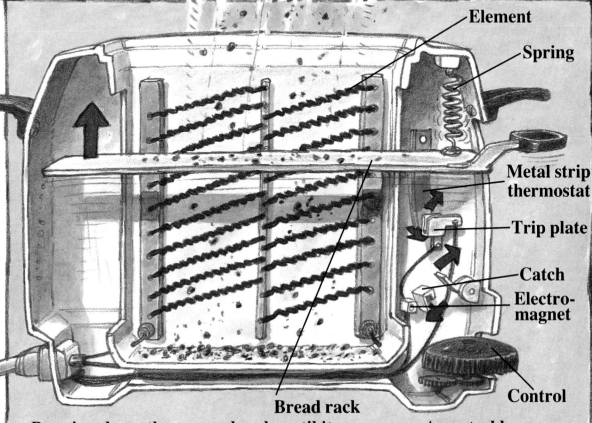

Element

Spring

Metal strip thermostat

Trip plate

Catch

Electro-magnet

Control

Bread rack

Pressing down the bread rack turns on the elements in a toaster.

The rack is pushed down against a spring and is held down by a catch.

In some toasters, as the bread heats up, a metal strip slowly

bends until it touches a "trip plate."

This switches on an *electromagnet,* which pulls the catch back, releasing the rack. The spring makes the rack pop up, turning off the elements.

A control lever moves the trip plate nearer to or farther from the metal strip. This sets the amount of time it takes for the strip to touch the plate, which makes the toast lighter or darker.

Cooling off

The refrigerator

The refrigerator keeps food cold by moving heat from inside the food compartment to outside. It works by turning a liquid into a gas (evaporation), and then turning the gas back into a liquid (condensation).

Molecules evaporating from a liquid need enough energy to escape. This energy can only come from the molecules left behind in the liquid. As a result, these lose energy, so the liquid becomes colder.

A refrigerator cannot work well with the door open, so it should always be shut quickly.

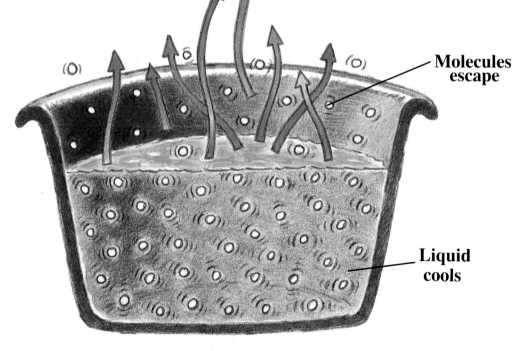

Molecules escape

Liquid cools

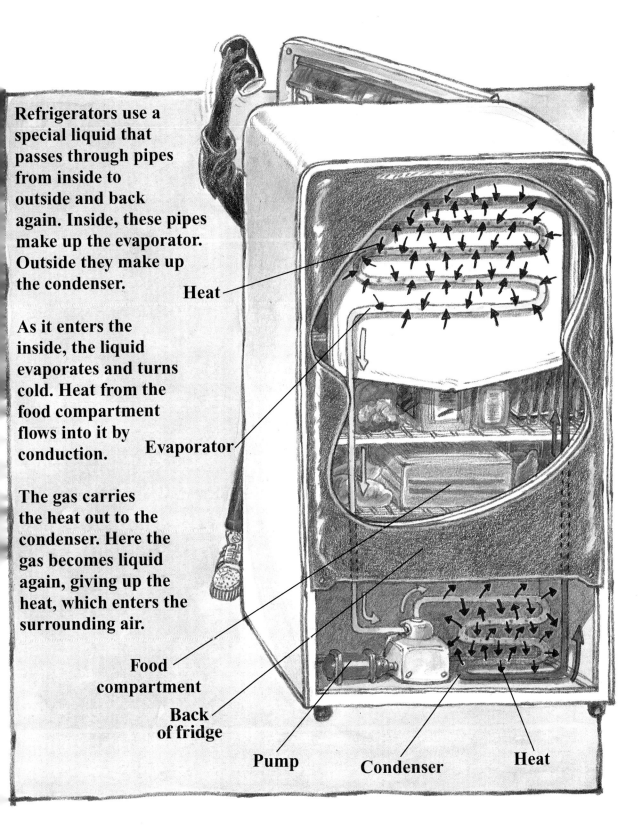

Refrigerators use a special liquid that passes through pipes from inside to outside and back again. Inside, these pipes make up the evaporator. Outside they make up the condenser.

As it enters the inside, the liquid evaporates and turns cold. Heat from the food compartment flows into it by conduction.

The gas carries the heat out to the condenser. Here the gas becomes liquid again, giving up the heat, which enters the surrounding air.

Heat

Evaporator

Food compartment

Back of fridge

Pump

Condenser

Heat

Insulation and the thermos

How far heat travels depends on what it is traveling through. Most metals conduct heat very well; heat spreads through them easily. There are many other materials—like plastic, wood, or rubber—that conduct heat badly. They are called *insulators*.

Air is an extremely good insulator. Moving air carries heat by convection, but air that has been trapped will not conduct heat.

Materials that trap air, like wool, cotton, or Styrofoam, make good insulators. It is not the wool itself in your sweater that keeps you warm, but the air that has been trapped by the wool threads.

Houses are insulated with foam, fiberglass, or Styrofoam-like materials to keep heat from escaping. Water pipes are insulated to keep them warm in winter, so the water will not freeze and then burst the pipes.

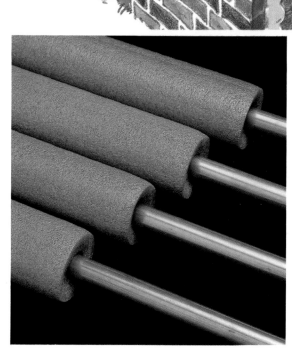

Plastic foam is wrapped around pipes to keep them warm.

The thermos

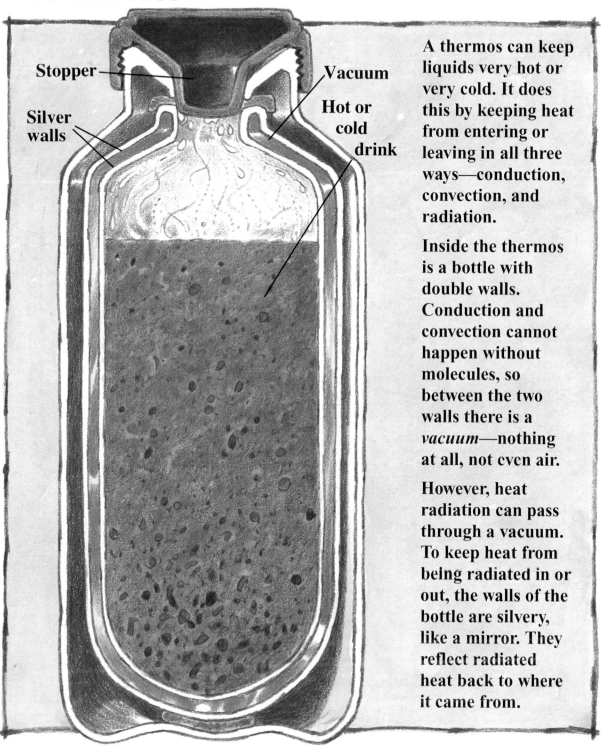

Stopper

Silver walls

Vacuum

Hot or cold drink

A thermos can keep liquids very hot or very cold. It does this by keeping heat from entering or leaving in all three ways—conduction, convection, and radiation.

Inside the thermos is a bottle with double walls. Conduction and convection cannot happen without molecules, so between the two walls there is a *vacuum*—nothing at all, not even air.

However, heat radiation can pass through a vacuum. To keep heat from being radiated in or out, the walls of the bottle are silvery, like a mirror. They reflect radiated heat back to where it came from.

Heat in industry

The blast furnace

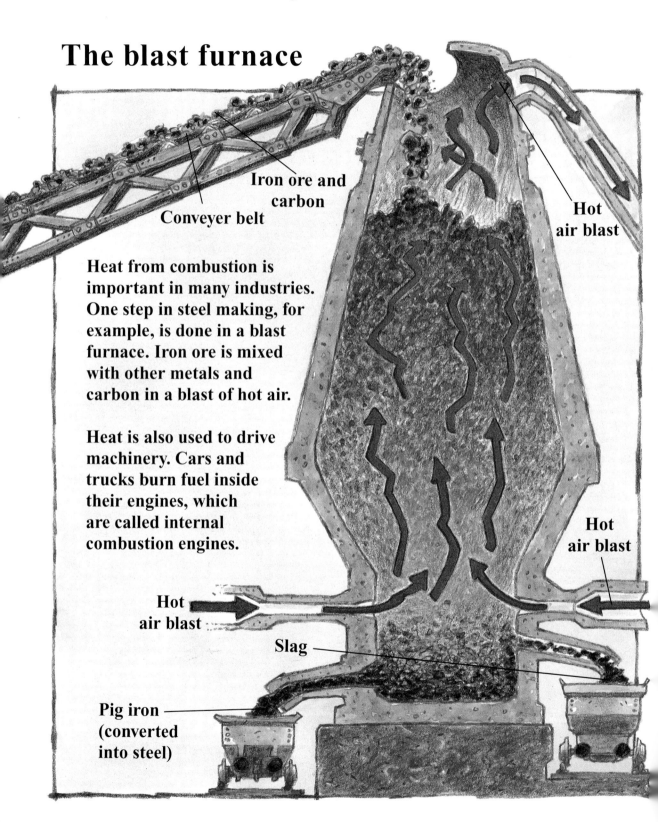

Iron ore and carbon

Conveyer belt

Hot air blast

Heat from combustion is important in many industries. One step in steel making, for example, is done in a blast furnace. Iron ore is mixed with other metals and carbon in a blast of hot air.

Heat is also used to drive machinery. Cars and trucks burn fuel inside their engines, which are called internal combustion engines.

Hot air blast

Hot air blast

Slag

Pig iron (converted into steel)

The steam engine

The steam engine was invented in the eighteenth century and played an important part in the *Industrial Revolution*.

The first steam engines burned coal for heat to boil water, which makes steam. The steam was then used to drive trains or power machinery.

Steam engines are rarely used anymore, but steam *turbine*s still make most household electricity.

High-pressure steam turns the turbine blades, changing heat energy into movement. This movement is used to generate electricity.

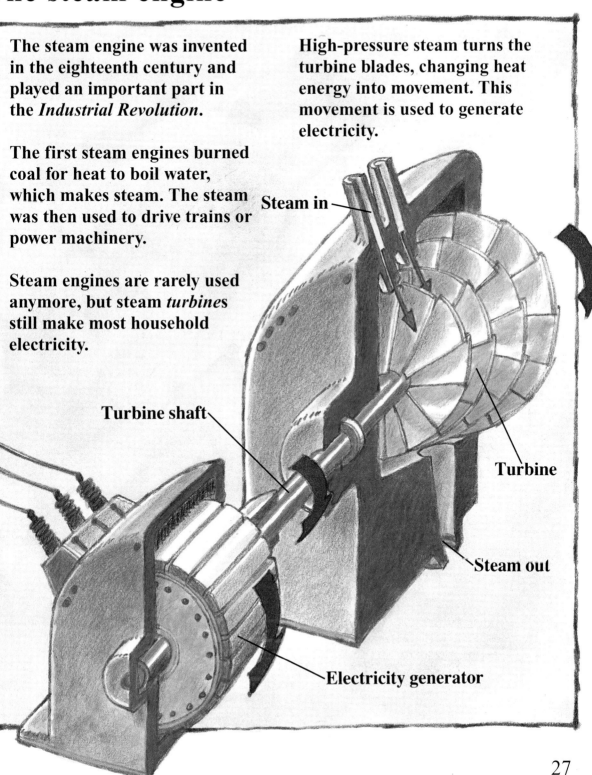

Steam in

Turbine shaft

Turbine

Steam out

Electricity generator

Heat and the sun

Millions of years ago, the plants that lived on Earth were soaking up energy from sunshine. Over the years, these plants rotted and slowly turned into coal and oil. We can release the sun's energy by burning these fuels, but we can also use energy from the sun directly.

Solar water heater

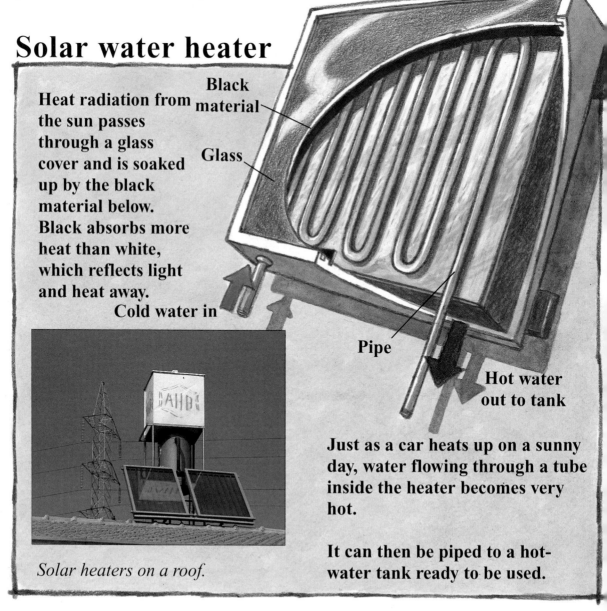

Heat radiation from the sun passes through a glass cover and is soaked up by the black material below. Black absorbs more heat than white, which reflects light and heat away.

Black material

Glass

Cold water in

Pipe

Hot water out to tank

Just as a car heats up on a sunny day, water flowing through a tube inside the heater becomes very hot.

It can then be piped to a hot-water tank ready to be used.

Solar heaters on a roof.

The human heater

Did you know that your body acts like a heater? It burns the food you eat to give you energy and keep you warm. Any spare energy is radiated away. Walking into a cold room is like turning on a small space heater.

Glossary

Acetylene   A poisonous gas that burns with a bright, hot flame.

Atoms   The tiny particles of which all things are made.

Combustion   The process of burning something in the air, in which part of the substance combines with oxygen.

Electromagnet   A magnet is an object that can pull things made of certain metals toward it. An electromagnet is a magnet made by coiling wire around a piece of iron or steel and sending an electric current through the wire. Its magnetism can be turned on and off.

Electrons   Tiny particles found inside all atoms. They are very small and carry electricity.

Elements   The parts of heaters, ovens, and stoves that heat up. Usually they are made of wire, and electricity is passed through them. In a gas heater the element is made of a hard clay that glows red-hot, radiating heat.

Energy   The power needed to do something.

Fuel   A substance such as coal or oil that can be burned to get energy in the form of heat.

Industrial Revolution   The period in the eighteenth and nineteenth centuries when many countries developed new industries. Many people stopped working on farms and went to work at the new factories in towns.

Insulator   Something that keeps heat from moving from one place to another.

Molecule   A clump of two or more atoms joined together.

Pollution   Anything that spoils our soil, water, or air. Polluted places are dirty and can be harmful to animals and plants.

Rays   Waves of energy carrying heat or light. Heat and light radiate from the sun and travel to Earth in rays.

Turbines   Machines that use the power of steam, gas, or water to make blades and a shaft turn around.

Vacuum   A space with nothing in it, not even air.

Vibrate   To move back and forth very quickly.

Welding   The process of joining two pieces of metal by heating them until they are soft, then holding them together until they cool and harden.

Books to read

Bailey, Donna. *What We Can Do About Conserving Energy.*
What We Can Do About. New York: Franklin Watts, 1992.

Catherall, Ed. *Exploring Energy Sources.*
Austin: Raintree Steck-Vaughn, 1991.

Cross, Wilbur. *Solar Energy.*
Science and Technology. Chicago: Childrens Press, 1984.

Jennings, Terry. *Hot and Cold.*
Junior Science. New York: Gloucester, 1989.

Parker, Steven. *The Random House Book of How Things Work.*
New York: Random House, 1991.

Rawson, Christopher. *How Machines Work.*
Tulsa, Okla: EDC, 1976.

Whyman, Kathryn. *Heat and Energy.*
Science Today. New York: Gloucester, 1986.

Picture acknowledgments

The publishers would like to thank the following for providing the photographs for this book: Eye Ubiquitous 12 (T. Futter), 18 (R. Chester), 24; Science Photo Library 28 (A. Bartel); Sefton Photo Library 11, 16; Tony Stone Worldwide 4, 9; Zefa 22 (C. Voigt).

Index